The Fabulous Life of Minnie the Sassy Chick:
Minnie's Sassy Birthday

To: Kalani

I hope this silly story makes you giggle :)

This is dedicated to my
fabulous and sassy niece's,
Carly and Riley.

Love and hugs always,
Aunt Cindy

Text copyright © Cindy Shirley, 2018.
Illustrations copyright © Cindy Shirley, 2018.
Edited by Cailey Shirley, 2018.
All rights reserved. No part of this book may be used or reproduced by any means, graphic, electronic, or mechanical, including photocopying, recording, taping or by any information storage retrieval system without the written permission of the publisher except in the case of brief quotations embodied in critical articles and reviews.

ISBN: Softcover 978-0-9986480-7-1
0-9986480-7-8
Hardcover 978-0-9986480-8-8
0-9986480-8-6

For other wonderful books by author Cindy L.Shirley, visit her at:
www.amazon.com/author/cindyshirley

Published by
Let's Pretend Publishing LLC

The Fabulous Life of Minnie the Sassy Chick:
Minnie's Sassy Birthday

Written by
Cindy L. Shirley

Illustrations by
Cleoward Sy

It's almost party time! Minnie the Sassy Chick will be celebrating her first birthday tomorrow. The two sisters, Carly and Riley, have a big surprise party planned for her.

"Our little chick has grown into a beautiful hen," declared Carly. "She sure is gorgeous with her long black eyelashes and fluffy pink feathers!" agreed Riley. The girls loved Minnie and made sure that her every want and need was taken care of. She was their best friend!

Riley and Minnie still spent their days pretending to be rock stars. Minnie was now old enough to really have some fun! After being dressed in proper attire, the radio was cranked up and the dancing began. Riley's favorite music was rock and roll, and she liked it loud! "We look too cool for school," shouted Riley over the blaring radio.

Minnie's beautiful pink feathers were very long now, and Riley loved to separate them into pig tails. She thought it was the most adorable thing she had ever seen.

Being silly, Riley would put her hair in pig tails too. "Look Minnie, we are twins!" she giggled.

Another part of their daily routine was to play beauty shop! Riley had watched her mom put on makeup every morning and thought she'd give it a try. "I like to use lots of pink eye shadow, blush and bright red lipstick," Riley whispered to Minnie as they sat there with makeup smeared all over their faces.

Minnie would stand in front of Riley's full-length mirror and stare lovingly at her reflection. Pleased with her appearance, she would begin cooing and fluff her feathers while batting her long eyelashes. "Oh, miss diva, you look fabulous!" laughed Riley.

At night after dinner, Carly would take Minnie back to her room and play spa party before going to bed. "You poor thing, you have got to be stressed out after being with Riley all day," sighed Carly. "It's time to sit back and relax!" Carly borrowed her mom's foot spa (which she always overfilled with soap), and found a small bowl for Minnie to use.

It wasn't long before Minnie began trying to peck at her tiara and all of the other bubbles around her. "That is no way to treat your tiara, young lady!" giggled Carly.

During bath time, Minnie loved to flap her wings and splash water all over the floor. What a mess Minnie could make! "Hey, calm down sassy chick! Let's get that makeup off your face and get you out of here!" Carly would shout.

With Minnie wrapped in a soft towel, Carly would use a blow dryer to dry her beautiful long feathers.

The warm air felt so good to Minnie that she usually fell asleep in Carly's arms. Afterwards, Minnie was always carried to bed and kissed goodnight. "I love you to the moon and back my sweet Minnie," Carly would whisper.

Finally, the day arrived to celebrate Minnie's birthday. The entire living room had been decorated with pink streamers, purple balloons and a bright pink rug to use for a runway. It was perfect for the special event they had planned! Their parents were very excited and already sitting on the couch waiting patiently for the fun to begin.

Happy Birthday Minnie

The girls had borrowed their mom's makeup to use for a fun-filled fashion show. Once they were dressed, they began helping Minnie get ready. "Ladies and gentlemen, our show will begin in just a few minutes!" announced Carly.

Just before the show started, the girls and Minnie all lined up. Each one was dressed to impress. Outrageous as always, Riley had used way too much lipstick, while Carly's purple eye shadow was halfway up her forehead. What a sight it was! After the girls finished a silly prance down the runway, they left a trail of cereal for Minnie to follow.

"Everybody, please give a big round of applause for the birthday princess herself, Miss Minnie the Sassy Chick!" announced Riley. "Woo hoo!" they all applauded as Minnie began to strut down the runway. She was wearing a pair of sparkle sunglasses, a pink feather boa, and a birthday princess tiara on top of her head. Just as she reached the end of the runway, she suddenly spun around and gave her tail feather a little shake. "Oh! my goodness!" snickered their mom.

"Wow! That bright red lipstick really brings out her beak, don't you think?" asked Carly. Smiling, her parents agreed and gave Minnie a standing ovation. "You girls look marvelous! I especially like what you've done with her feathers, Riley," chuckled their Dad.

Minnie began squawking, "cluck, cluck, cluck", as she strutted wildly around the room while batting her eyes. The girls laughed hysterically and each took a bow.

"So, what would you silly girls like for lunch on this special occasion?" asked their mom. "Cluck, cluck, cluck," answered Minnie. "That means spaghetti!" declared Carly. "That sounds yummy", said their mom as she chuckled and walked into the kitchen. "Lunch will be ready in a jiffy!"

With Minnie by their side, they all sat down at the table. Carly loved to eat her spaghetti noodles with lots of strawberry jelly instead of spaghetti sauce. "How disgusting, Carly!" scoffed Riley. "I wish you would just eat normal spaghetti sauce for a change." This only made Carly grin and use more jelly than usual. She loved to gross out her big sister whenever possible.

Their mom gave them each a glass of milk and put a big pile of noodles on both of their plates before she realized that Minnie was now standing on the table eating the noodles too. "Oh gross," said Riley, "It looks like she's eating worms!" There stood Minnie with noodles hanging out of both sides of her beak. Carly laughed so hard that she choked on her milk and spit it out everywhere. Minnie was still wearing her sunglasses, boa, and tiara, which made her look hilarious! Riley was laughing so hard that she had tears pouring down her face.

Minnie tilted her head sideways and looked at the girls while batting her long eyelashes. "Cluck, cluck?" she squawked. "Stop it, stop it, I can't catch my breath!" cried Riley. By now, the girls had both slid out of their chairs and were on the floor laughing uncontrollably. Minnie, not wanting to be left out, jumped down from the table and began splashing in the puddle of spilled milk. "Good grief, just look at this mess!" exclaimed their mom. It was such a funny sight that all she could do was shake her head and laugh.

"Okay silly girls, go ahead and get back in your seats so we can sing happy birthday to miss Minnie. After that, you can all have a piece of birthday cake!" said their dad cheerfully, as he lit the candle on Minnie's cake.

After drying Minnie's feet, Riley helped her back into her chair and then sat down across from Carly. The girls were still laughing about how ridiculous Minnie looked. "All together now!" said their mom. Everyone then began to sing. *"Happy birthday to you, happy birthday to you, happy birthday dear Minnie, happy birthday to you! And many more!"* "Make a wish!" cheered the girls. Suddenly, Minnie let out a powerful sneeze that blew out the candle on her cake. The sneeze was so strong that it made her tiara fall off her head and land on her beak. Laughing at how goofy she looked, everyone applauded and shouted hooray!

"One thing is for sure; you girls are definitely the silliest and sassiest chicks I have ever seen!" said their mom. "And you, Miss Minnie, have a crazy future ahead of you with these two in charge!"

For other wonderful books by author Cindy L.Shirley, visit her at:
www.amazon.com/author/cindyshirley

Made in the USA
Columbia, SC
08 April 2021